QuickStudy®

for

Spanish

BarCharts, Inc.®

Boca Raton, Florida

©2006 BarCharts, Inc.
ISBN 13: 9781423202554
ISBN 10: 1423202554

BarCharts® and QuickStudy® are registered trademarks of BarCharts, Inc.

Publisher:

       BarCharts, Inc.
       6000 Park of Commerce Boulevard, Suite D
       Boca Raton, FL 33487
       www.quickstudy.com

Printed in Thailand

Contents

Study Hints

NOTE TO STUDENT:
Use this QuickStudy® booklet to make the most of your studying time.

QuickStudy® notes provide need-to-know information; read them carefully to better understand key concepts.

> **NOTES**
> The masculine singular form of the definite article, **el**, is used before certain feminine nouns that begin with stressed **a**: **el águila** (eagle), **el agua** (water)

QuickStudy® examples offer detailed explanations; refer to them often to avoid problems.

> *Examples:*
> - Mr. García traveled to the United States on May 2, 1993.
>   **El señor García viajó a los Estados Unidos el 2 de mayo de 1993**.

Take your learning to the next level with QuickStudy®!

The Alphabet

NOTES
There are 30 letters in the Spanish alphabet.

a	a		**n**	ene
b	be		**ñ**	eñe
c	ce		**o**	o
ch	che		**p**	pe
d	de		**q**	cu
e	e		**r**	ere
f	efe		**rr**	erre
g	ge		**s**	ese
h	hache		**t**	te
i	i		**u**	u
j	jota		**v**	ve
k	ka		**w**	doble ve
l	ele		**x**	equis
ll	elle		**y**	i griega
m	eme		**z**	zeta

2 **Pronunciation**

a	=	ah	
ai	=	ahy	
au	=	ow	
o	=	oh	
e	=	eh	
ei	=	ay	
i	=	ee	
ia	=	yah	
ie	=	yeh	
io	=	yoh	
u	=	oo	
ua	=	wah	
ue	=	weh	
ll	=	ye	like in **y**am
ñ	=	nye	like in ca**ny**on
qu	=	k	like in **k**eep
rr	=	rrrr	(with a strong trill)
cc	=	ks	like in a**cc**ept

3 **Rules of Stress**

■ When a word ends in a vowel, **n** or **s,** the stress falls on the next to the last syllable: **ca ba llo** (horse), **e xa men** (exam), **e llos** (they).

■ When a word ends in a consonant, except **n** or **s,** the stress falls in the last syllable: **es pa ñol** (Spanish), **ciu dad** (city).

■ When the pronunciation of a word does not conform to any of the above rules, a written accent is required to indicate which syllable to stress: **ca fé** (coffee), **ár bol** (tree).

■ Sometimes written accents are used to differentiate two words with the same spelling:
◆ **tú** (you, familiar, subject pronoun) and **tu** (your, possessive adjective).
◆ **dé** (verb to give) and **de** (preposition)
◆ **sí** (yes) **si** (if)
◆ Certain pronouns such as **que, quien(es), cual(es), cuanto(a), cuantos(as)** and certain adverbs such as **cuando** and **donde,** when used as interrogatives, require a written accent: **¿Cuándo vas a estudiar? ¿Quiénes vienen?**

4 Syllables

■ Two or three vowels in Spanish can blend together to form a **diphthong** or a **triphthong.**
   ◆ Diphthongs and triphthongs are considered single vowels and cannot be divided: **es-tu-dian-te** (student); **a-bue-la** (grandmother).

■ Two strong vowels (a, e, o) do not form a diphthong and are separated into two syllables: **em-ple-o** (job); **re-a-li-dad** (reality).

■ A written accent on a weak vowel **(i, u)** breaks a diphthong:
   ◆ Thus the vowels are separated into two syllables: **re-ú-ne** (reunite); **dí-a** (day).

■ A single consonant forms a syllable with the vowel that follows it: **mu-ñe-ca** (doll); **za-pa-tos** (shoes).

NOTES
Double "r" (rr) and double "l" (ll) are considered single consonants: pe-rro (dog); ma-lla (net).

■ When two consonants appear between two vowels, they are separated into syllables: **mar-tes** (Tuesday); **car-ta** (letter).

◆ Exceptions: **b, c, d, f, g, p** or **t** followed by **l** or **r**: **cla-se** (class); **a-pren-der** (to learn).

■ When three consonants appear between two vowels, only the last one is included in the following syllable: **ins-ti-tu-to** (institute); **trans-fe-rir** (to transfer).

◆ Exceptions: **b, c, d, f, g, p,** or **t** followed by **l** or **r**: **hom-bre** (man); **In-gla-te-rra** (England).

5 Capitalization

NOTES
Only the first word in a sentence and proper nouns (i.e., countries, continents and persons) are capitalized.

Examples:
- Mr. García traveled to the United States on May 2, 1993.
  El señor García viajó a los Estados Unidos el 2 de mayo de 1993.

■ Nouns and adjectives that denote nationality, religious affiliation, names of languages, months of the year, and days of the week are generally **not** capitalized.

Numerals

Cardinals

0	**cero**
1	**un(o)**
2	**dos**
3	**tres**
4	**cuatro**
5	**cinco**
6	**seis**
7	**siete**
8	**ocho**
9	**nueve**
10	**diez**
11	**once**
12	**doce**
13	**trece**
14	**catorce**
15	**quince**
16	**dieciséis**
17	**diecisiete**
18	**dieciocho**
19	**diecinueve**

20	veinte
21	veintiúno
22	veintidós
23	veintitrés
30	treinta
31	treinta y uno
32	treinta y dos
33	treinta y tres
40	cuarenta
41	cuarenta y uno
42	cuarenta y dos
43	cuarenta y tres
50	cincuenta
60	sesenta
70	setenta
71	setenta y uno
80	ochenta
90	noventa
91	noventa y uno
100	cien (to)
200	doscientos
201	doscientos uno
300	trescientos/as
400	cuatrocientos/as
500	quinientos/as
600	seiscientos/as

700	**setecientos/as**
800	**ochocientos/as**
900	**novecientos/as**

1,000	**mil**
2,000	**dos mil**
1,000,000	**un millón (de)**
2,000,000	**dos millones (de)**

| million | **millón** |
| billion | **mil millones** |

NOTES

Uno, or any number ending in **uno**, drops the final **o** when followed by a masculine noun: **un libro, veintiún profesores**.

Ordinals

first	(1st)	**primero**	(1°)
second	(2nd)	**segundo**	(2°)
third	(3rd)	**tercero**	(3°)
fourth	(4th)	**cuarto**	(4°)
fifth	(5th)	**quinto**	(5°)
sixth	(6th)	**sexto**	(6°)
seventh	(7th)	**séptimo**	(7°)
eighth	(8th)	**octavo**	(8°)
ninth	(9th)	**noveno**	(9°)
tenth	(10th)	**décimo**	(10°)
eleventh	(11th)	**undécimo**	(11°)
twentieth	(20th)	**vigésimo**	(20°)

(the) first	**(el/la) primero/a**
(the) last	**(el/la) último/a**
(the) second	**(el/la) segundo/a**

7 Nouns

Gender

■ Most nouns ending in **-o** are masculine: **el libro** (the book), but there are exceptions such as **la mano** (the hand), **la moto** (the motorcycle).

◆ Some nouns ending in **-ma** and referring to non-concrete things are masculine: **el clima** (the climate), **el drama** (the drama), **el idioma** (the language), **el poeta** (the poet), **el problema** (the problem), **el programa** (the program), **el sistema** (the system), **el tema** (the theme).

■ Most nouns ending in **-a** are feminine: **la mesa** (the table), with exceptions such as **el mapa** (the map), **el día** (the day).

◆ Nouns ending in **ión, -dad, -tad, -tud, -umbre** are feminine: **la estación** (the season), **la opresión** (the oppression) **la ciudad** (the city), **la libertad** (the freedom), **la juventud** (the youth), **la muchedumbre** (the crowd).

Plural

■ If a noun ends in:
- ◆ a vowel, add **-s: libro/libros, puerta/puertas**
- ◆ a consonant, add **-es: pared/paredes, profesor/ profesores**
- ◆ **-z,** change it to a **-c** and add **-es: lápiz/lápices, luz/luces**

Articles

NOTES
Articles must agree in gender and number with the noun that they accompany.

Definite Articles
■ [el, la, los, las (the)] are used:
  ◆ With infinitives used as nouns, particularly at beginning of a sentence: **El estudiar es bueno.** (Studying is good.)
  ◆ With nouns listed in a series: **Pongo el libro, el cuaderno y la pluma sobre la mesa.** (I am putting the book, the notebook and the pen on the table.)
  ◆ With certain nouns such as **escuela, corte, cárcel,** with which articles are omitted in English: **Los ladrones van a la cárcel.** (Thieves go to jail.); **Los chicos aprenden mucho en la escuela.** (Children learn a lot in school.)
  ◆ To identify an intangible concept: **La bondad es una virtud.** (Kindness is a virtue.)
  ◆ To identify something specific that precedes a demonstrative adjective: **El muchacho éste no tiene dinero.** (This young man does not have [any] money.)

17

◆ With a noun of weight or measure: **Las naranjas cuestan un dólar la libra.** (Oranges cost one dollar per pound.)

◆ With titles, ranks, and professions when used with a proper name: **La doctora García llamó.** (Dr. García called.)

◆ With the name of a subject: **Estudio la historia.** (I study history.)

◆ With days of the week to indicate when something occurs, where we use "on" in English: **A veces vamos al cine el sábado**. (Sometimes we go to the movies on Saturday.)

◆ With parts of the body or articles of clothing, especially if the possessor is clearly indicated as in the case of reflexive verbs: **Me pongo el abrigo.** (I am putting on my coat.)

◆ With the seasons of the year: **En la primavera llueve mucho.** (In spring it rains a lot.)

◆ To show possession: **El abrigo de mi hermano está en el armario.** (My brother's coat is in the closet.)

◆ With names of certain cities, countries, and continents: **la Argentina, los Estados Unidos, la Habana, la América del Sur.**

◆ With a proper noun modified by an adjective: **el pequeño José** (Little Joseph).

◆ With a noun in apposition with a pronoun: **Nosotros los norteamericanos** (We North Americans).

◆ With the hour (preceding it) when telling time: **Es la una.** (It is one o'clock.)

NOTES
The masculine singular form of the definite article, el, is used before certain feminine nouns that begin with stressed a: el águila (eagle), el agua (water).

Indefinite Articles

■ **un, una, unos, unas** (a, some) normally precede a noun.
   ◆ In specific cases an article is not used
      • After a form of the verb **ser** (to be) when the noun following it is not modified: **Soy profesora.** NOT **Soy una buena profesora.**

Pronouns

> **NOTES**
> Pronouns are words that replace nouns.

Personal Pronouns

	As subject	As indirect object	As direct object
yo	I	**me** to me	**me** me
tú	you (fam.)	**te** to you (fam.)	**te** you (fam.)
él	he	**le** to him, to her, to you (form.)	**lo** him, it, you (masc.)
ella	she		**la** her, it, you (fem.)
usted	you (form.)		
nosotros (-as) we		**nos** to us	**nos** (us)
vosotros (-as) you (fam.)		**os** to you (fam.)	**os** you (fam.)
ellos	they (masc.)	**les** to them, to you (form.)	**los** them, you (masc.)
ellas	they (fem.)		**las** them, you (fem.)
ustedes	you (form.)		

> *Examples:*
> Here is a key to abbreviations used throughout this book:
> **(fam.)** = familiar/informal
> **(form.)** = formal/polite
> **(masc.)** = masculine
> **(fem.)** = feminine
> **(sing.)** = singular
> **(pl.)** = plural

Other Pronouns

■ **Possessive**

◆ Formed by using the appropriate definite article (el, los, la, las) plus a long form of the possessive given below.

◆ Agrees in gender and number with the noun it replaces: **Mi hermana es más alta que la tuya.** (My sister is taller than yours.)

singular-m/f	plural-m/f	
el mío, la mía	**los míos, las mías**	mine
el tuyo, la tuya	**los tuyos, las tuyas**	yours (fam.sing.)
el suyo, la suya	**los suyos, las suyas**	yours (formal)
		his, hers, its
el nuestro,	**los nuestros,**	ours
la nuestra	**las nuestras**	
el vuestro,	**los vuestros,**	yours (fam.pl.)
la vuestra	**las vuestras**	
el suyo, la suya	**los suyos, las suyas**	yours, theirs (formal)

■ **Demonstrative**

masc.	fem.	neuter	
éste	**ésta**	**esto**	this one (here)
éstos	**éstas**		these (here)
ése	**ésa**	**eso**	that one (there)
ésos	**ésas**		those (there)
aquél	**aquélla**	**aquello**	that on (over there)
aquéllos	**aquéllas**		those (over there)

Nosotros queremos ver estas blusas y aquéllas. (We want to see these blouses and those over there.)

■ **Relative**

◆ Connect the subordinate clause with an antecedent in the main clause.

- ◆ Relative pronouns are never omitted in Spanish.
- ◆ **Que** is the most common relative pronoun and is invariable in form.
  - It may refer to both people and things, regardless of gender and number.
  - It may also be used as a subject or an object.
- ◆ **Quien, quienes** (who, whom) refer only to people.
  - **Quien** is normally used after the prepositions **a, de, con** and **en**.

■ Interrogative
- ◆ **¿qué?** (what?)
- ◆ **¿cuál? ¿cuáles?** (what? which?)
- ◆ **¿cuánto? ¿cuánta?** (how much?)
- ◆ **¿cuántos? ¿cuántas?** (how many?)
- ◆ **¿quién? ¿quiénes?** (who?)

■ Reflexive
- ◆ Used to conjugate reflexive verbs:

singular		plural	
me	myself	**nos**	ourselves
te	yourself (familiar)	**os**	yourselves (familiar)
se	himself, herself; yourself (formal)	**se**	themselves; yourselves (formal)

Position of Direct & Indirect Object Pronouns

■ Before the verb if it is:
- ◆ A conjugated verb: **Ella lo estudia.** (She studies it.); **Elena nos ve.** (Elena sees us.)
  - Exception to this rule is affirmative imperative, in which case the object pronoun follows (and is attached to) the verb: **Dígame** (Tell me); **Cómalo** (Eat it).

■ **After** (attached to) **the verb** if it is:
  ◆ An infinitive: **Quiero comerlo.** (I want to eat it.)
  ◆ A present participle: **Estoy estudiándolo.** (I am studying it.)

Examples:
A pronoun may precede a conjugated verb or follow an infinitive or a present participle:
Lo quiero comer.
Quiero comerlo.
Estoy estudiándolo.
Lo estoy estudiando.

■ **Direct and indirect object pronouns together:**
  ◆ When two object pronouns appear in a sentence, the indirect object pronoun precedes the direct object pronoun: **David te lo dio.** (David gave it to you.)
  ◆ If both pronouns are in the third person, **le, les** are replaced by **se: Se lo escribiré or Voy a escribírselo.** (I write it to him, her, you, singular or plural, to them, feminine or masculine plural.)
  ◆ Since **"se"** may mean to him, to her, to them, to you, etc., you can add **a** plus the prepositional pronoun form to clarify: **a él, a ella, a usted, a ustedes, a ellos, a ellas: La madre se los compra [a ellos].** (The mother buys it for them.)

As Objects of Preposition

Pronouns used with a preposition are the same as the subject pronouns, except for the first and second persons singular and the reflexive "sí."

singular		plural	
mí	me	**nosotros**	us
ti	you (familiar)	**vosotros**	you (familiar)
él	him	**ellos**	them (masculine)
ella	her	**ellas**	them (feminine)
usted	you (formal)	**ustedes**	you (formal)

With **con: mí, ti, sí** become **conmigo, contigo, consigo**

Adjectives

NOTES
Adjectives modify (describe) nouns and pronouns.

■ Adjectives must agree in gender and number with the noun they modify:
  ◆ Most masculine adjectives end in -o
  ◆ Most feminine adjectives end in **-a**
  ◆ Most adjectives that do not end in **-o** or **-a** use the same form for both the feminine and the masculine: gentil, amable
  ◆ Adjectives ending in **-án** and **-ón** are made feminine by adding **-a** and dropping the accent: bonachón-bonachona
  ◆ Adjectives ending in **-d** or **-r** are made feminine by adding **-a: encantador - encantadora**
  ◆ Adjectives of nationality ending in a consonant are made feminine by adding **-a** and dropping the accent (if there is one): **alemán - alemana**
  ◆ Adjectives are made plural the same way as nouns:
    • Adjectives that modify two or more nouns of different gender are normally masculine plural.
■ **Descriptive Adjectives**
  ◆ Generally follow the nouns they modify: **el libro interesante** (the interesting book); **la casa blanca** (the white house).

◆ If, however, the adjective does not add a distin-
guishing characteristic or emphasis, but rather
readily associates with the noun, descriptive
adjectives will frequently precede the noun: **la
blanca nieve** (the white snow).

■ **Limiting Adjectives**
◆ Demonstratives, possessives, and indefinite articles, cardinal numbers, and ordinal numbers
usually precede the noun: **estas camisas** (these
shirts); **mis amigos** (my friends); **muchos
dólares** (many dollars); **siete coches** (seven
cars); and **el quinto capítulo** (the fifth chapter).
◆ Certain adjectives normally precede the nouns
they modify and lose their final **-o** before a masculine singular noun: **un buen muchacho** (a
good boy); **el primer año** (the first year); **algún
día** (some day).

■ **Demonstrative Adjectives**

Masculine	Feminine
este libro this book	**esta pluma** this pen
estos libros these books	**estas plumas** these pens
ese libro	**esa pluma**
that book near you	that pen near you
esos libros	**esas plumas**
those books near you	those pens near you
[indicate farther distance from speaker]	
aquel libro	**aquella pluma**
that book over there	that pen over there
aquellos libros	**aquellas plumas**
those books over there	those pens over there

■ Possessive Adjectives

Masculine

mi coche my car
mis coches my cars
tu coche your car (fam.)
tus coches your cars (fam.)

su coche his car; her car; your car (formal); their car

sus coches his cars; her cars; your cars (formal); their cars

nuestro coche our car
nuestros coches our cars
vuestro coche your car (fam.)
vuestros coches your cars (fam.)

Feminine

mi casa my house
mis casas my houses
tu casa your house (fam.)
tus casas your houses (fam.)

su casa his house; her house, your house (formal); their house

sus casas his houses; her houses; your houses (formal); their houses

nuestra casa our house
nuestras casas our houses
vuestra casa your house (fam.)
vuestras casas your houses (fam.)

Common Adjectives

Add "s" for plurals. If a plural is irregular, the plural form is indicated in parentheses.

adorable	**adorable**
affectionate	**cariñoso/a**
aged	**viejo/a**
ambitious	**ambicioso/a**
ancient	**antiguo/a**
angry	**enfadado/a**
anxious	**preocupado/a**
ashamed	**avergonzado/a**
athletic	**atlético/a**
beautiful	**hermoso/a**
big	**grande**

blond	**rubio/a**
brunette	**morena**
calm	**quieto/a**
comfortable	**confortable**
cute	**lindo/a**
delighted	**encantado/a**
difficult	**difícil(es)**
disciplined	**disciplinado/a**
divorced	**divorciado/a**
eccentric	**excéntrico/a**
elegant	**elegante**
energetic	**enérgico/a**
engaged	**prometido/a**
faithful	**fiel(es)**
fantastic	**fantástico/a**
fat	**gordo/a**
first	**primero/a**
funny	**gracioso/a**
furious	**furioso/a**
furnished	**amueblado/a**
generous	**generoso/a**
gentle	**gentil(es)**
gifted	**talentoso/a**
good	**bueno/a**
happy	**feliz (felices)**
idealist	**idealista**
in love	**enamorado/a**
irritable	**irritable**
jealous	**celoso/a**
large	**grande**
likable	**simpático/a**
married	**casado/a**
mean	**mezquino/a**
medium	**mediano/a**
modern	**moderno/a**
new	**nuevo/a**

nice/kind	**agradable/amable**
old	**viejo/a**
optimistic	**optimista**
pessimistic	**pesimista**
pleasant	**agradable**
polite	**cortés**
practical	**práctico/a**
pretty	**lindo/a**
reasonable	**razonable**
redhead	**pelirrojo/a**
reserved	**reservado/a**
sad	**triste**
selfish	**egoísta**
sensible	**razonable** _sensible_
sensitive	**impresionable** _sensitivo_
serious	**serio/a**
shy	**tímido/a**
short	**corto/a, bajo/a**
single	**solo/a**
sociable	**sociable**
stern	**severo/a**
strong	**fuerte**
strange	**extraño/a**
stressed	**estresado/a**
stupid	**estúpido/a**
stubborn	**testarudo/a** _terco_
super, great	**estupendo**
surprised	**sorprendido/a**
tall	**grande, alto/a**
tender	**delicado/a**
tiresome	**pesado/a**
unhappy	**desdichado/a**
well	**bien (sano/a)**
worn out (object)	**gastado/a**
worried	**preocupado/a**
young	**joven**

11 Comparatives & Superlatives

Comparatives

■ Inequality

◆ Formed by placing **más** or **menos** before and **que** after the adjective, adverb or noun: **Nélida es más baja que Elena.** (Nélida is shorter than Helen.); **Rosa canta menos frecuentemente que su hermana.** (Rosa sings less frequently than her sister.); **El chico tiene menos dinero que yo.** (The boy has less money than I.)

◆ Irregular forms: **bueno, mejor** (good, better); **malo, peor** (bad, worse); **grande, mayor** (big, bigger or older)

■ Equality

◆ Formed by using **tan** followed by an adjective or adverb plus **como: Isabel es tan inteligente como Lucía.** (Isabel is as intelligent as Lucía.)

• **Tanto** (os,a,as) is used with a noun: **Tengo tanto dinero como tú.** (I have as much money as you.)

Superlatives

■ The superlative is formed by placing a definite article and **"más"** or **"menos"** in front of an adjective: **Roberto es el chico más inteligente de la clase.** (Roberto is the most intelligent boy in the class.)

♦ "De" is used in this instance as the English equivalent of "in."

♦ The noun can be omitted: Roberto es el más inteligente de la clase.

12 Adverbs

NOTES

Adverbs modify (describe) verbs, adjectives or other adverbs.

■ To form an adverb add **-mente** to the feminine singular form of the adjective:
correcto = correctamente (correctly).
■ An adverb precedes the adjective it modifies but normally follows the verb it modifies:

Examples:
- The professor is very intelligent.
  La profesora es muy inteligente.
- Their pronunciation is good.
  Ellos pronuncian bien.

Common Adverbs

a lot	**mucho**
almost	**casi**
already	**ya**
also	**también**
always	**siempre**
as much	**tanto**
badly	**mal**

enough	**bastante**
late	**tarde**
little	**poco**
much	**mucho**
often	**a menudo**
quickly	**rápidamente**
rather	**bastante**
so much	**tanto**
sometimes	**a veces**
soon	**pronto**
still	**aún/todavía**
together	**juntos**
too much	**demasiado**
very	**muy**
well	**bien**

Prepositions

NOTES
Prepositions connect nouns or pronouns to other words.

Most Common Prepositions

a	at, to	**hacia**	toward
ante	before	**hasta**	until, up to
bajo	under	**para**	for, in order to
con	with	**por**	by, for
contra	against	**según**	according to
de	of, from	**sin**	without
desde	from, since	**sobre**	on
en	in	**tras**	behind

Many verbs require a preposition before an infinitive. (It is best to learn the verb along with the preposition.)

■ **"a"** (to)
  ◆ Verbs of commencement, motion, teaching, and learning must be followed by **a** before an infinitive: **aprender a, comenzar a, ir a,** etc.

■ **con** (with)
  ◆ Verbs that require **con** are: **contar con, soñar con**

■ **de** (from)
- ◆ Verbs that require **de** are: **acabar de, dejar de, olvidarse de, tratar de**

■ **en** (in)
- ◆ With **en: insistir en, tardar en**

■ **por** (for, through)
- ◆ With **por: preocuparse por**

Usage

■ personal "**a**"
- ◆ Spanish requires an "**a**" before a direct object that refers to a definite person or persons: **Tú ves a ese joven todos los días.** (You see that young man every day.)

■ **de** used to indicate possession
- ◆ **El libro de Juan es rojo.** (John's book is red.)

■ **para**
- ◆ Purpose, direction, destination or intention: **El estudia para abogado.** (He is studying to be a lawyer.)
- ◆ A time limit by which something is to be done: **Terminaré el proyecto para el lunes.** (I will finish the project by Monday.)
- ◆ In idiomatic expressions: **para siempre** (forever)

■ **por**
- ◆ Along or through, for, during a period of time, in exchange for, for the sake of, per, by means of: **Caminan por el parque.** (They walk through the park.) **Fueron a México por dos semanas.** (They went to Mexico for two weeks.)

◆ **Por** in idiomatic expressions: **por favor** (please), **por ejemplo** (for example), **por eso** (therefore)

Verbs
The Basics

Moods
■ **Indicative**
◆ Expresses facts and actual situations.

■ **Subjunctive**
◆ Used to express actions that are doubtful,
possible or wished for.

■ **Imperative**
◆ Used to express orders (commands).

Conjugations
■ **According to infinitive endings: -ar, -er, -ir**
◆ Most verb forms are created by dropping the
infinitive ending (leaving the infinitive stem)
and adding other endings.
◆ Verbs following these general formation rules
are called regular verbs.

■ **Different endings**

◆ Depend on mood, tense or person of verb (the infinitive, the present participle and the past participle do not change).

Regular Verbs
Formation of Simple Tenses (Indicative & Subjunctive Moods)

-ar ending: hablar = to speak
Pres. Part: habl + ando
Past. Part: habl + ado

		Singular			Plural		
Present	habl	o	as	a	amos	áis	an
Imperfect	habl	aba	abas	aba	ábamos	abais	aban
Preterit	habl	é	aste	ó	amos	asteis	aron
Future	hablar	é	ás	á	emos	éis	án
Conditional	hablar	ía	ías	ía	íamos	íais	ían
Pres. Subj.	habl	e	es	e	emos	éis	en
Imp. Subj.	habla	ra	ras	ra	ramos	rais	ran

-er ending: comer = to eat
Pres. Part: com + iendo
Past. Part: com + ido

		Singular			Plural		
Present	com	o	es	e	emos	éis en	
Imperfect	com	ía	ías	ía	íamos	íais	ían
Preterit	com	í	iste	ió	imos	isteis	ieron
Future	comer	é	ás	á	emos	éis	án
Conditional	comer	ía	ías	ía	íamos	íais	ían
Pres. Subj.	com	a	as	a	amos	áis	an
Imp. Subj.	comie	ra	ras	ra	ramos	rais	ran

-ir ending: vivir = to live
Pres. Part: viv + iendo
Past. Part: viv + ido

		Singular			Plural		
Present	viv	o	es	e	imos	ís	en
Imperfect	viv	ía	ías	ía	íamos	íais	ían
Preterit	viv	í	iste	ió	imos	isteis	ieron
Future	vivir	é	ás	á	emos	éis	án
Conditional	vivir	ía	ías	ía	íamos	íais	ían
Pres. Subj.	viv	a	as	a	amos	áis	an
Imp. Subj.	vivie	ra	ras	ra	ramos	rais	ran

Passive Voice

■ To express an indefinite subject, Spanish uses "**se**" with the third-person singular of a verb: **Se dice que te gusta el helado.** (It is said that you like ice cream.); **Se estudia mucho aquí.** (One studies very much here. OR People study very much here.)

■ If the subject is a thing, and the activator of the verb is not specified, "**se**" can be used in either the third-person singular or plural, depending on whether the subject is singular or plural: **Se habla inglés allí.** (English is spoken there.); **Se presenta el grupo hoy.** (The group is presented today.)

Irregular Verbs

> **NOTES**
> Spanish has many irregular verbs. Learning
> them will help you improve your Spanish.

Present Tense

■ **cocer:** cuezo, cueces, cuece, cocemos, cocéis,
cuecen

■ **coger:** cojo, coges, coge, cogemos, cogéis, cogen

■ **dar:** doy, das, da, damos, dais, dan

■ **decir:** digo, dices, dice, decimos, decís, dicen

■ **estar:** estoy, estás, está, estamos, estáis, están

■ **haber:** he, has, ha, hemos, habéis, han

■ **ir:** voy, vas, va, vamos, vais, van

■ **obtener:** obtengo, obtienes, obtiene, obtenemos,
obtenéis, obtienen

■ **oír:** oigo, oyes, oye, oímos, oís, oyen

■ **reír:** río, ríes, ríe, reímos, reís, ríen

■ **ser:** soy, eres, es, somos, sois, son

■ **sonreír:** sonrío, sonríes, sonríe, sonreímos,
sonreís, sonríen

■ **tener:** tengo, tienes, tiene, tenemos, tenéis, tienen

■ **venir:** vengo, vienes, viene, venimos, venís,
vienen

Verbs Irregular in the First Person Only

- ◆ **caber:** quepo
- ◆ **caer:** caigo
- ◆ **conducir:** conduzco
- ◆ **conocer:** conozco
- ◆ **dar:** doy
- ◆ **hacer:** hago
- ◆ **nacer:** nazco
- ◆ **poner:** pongo
- ◆ **saber:** sé
- ◆ **salir:** salgo
- ◆ **traer:** traigo
- ◆ **valer:** valgo
- ◆ **ver:** veo

Present Participles

- ■ **caer:** cayendo
- ■ **creer:** creyendo
- ■ **decir:** diciendo
- ■ **dormir:** durmiendo
- ■ **ir:** yendo
- ■ **leer:** leyendo
- ■ **mentir:** mintiendo
- ■ **morir:** muriendo
- ■ **oir:** oyendo
- ■ **pedir:** pidiendo
- ■ **poder:** pudiendo
- ■ **preferir:** prefiriendo
- ■ **reír:** riendo
- ■ **seguir:** siguiendo
- ■ **sentir:** sintiendo
- ■ **ser:** siendo
- ■ **servir:** sirviendo
- ■ **traer:** trayendo
- ■ **venir:** viniendo
- ■ Verbs that are rarely used in the present progressive:
  - ◆ estar
  - ◆ ir
  - ◆ ser
  - ◆ venir

Preterit Tense

- **andar:** anduve, anduviste, anduvo, anduvimos, anduvisteis, anduvieron
- **caber:** cupe, cupiste, cupo, cupimos, cupisteis, cupieron
- **caer:** caí, caíste, cayó, caímos, caísteis, cayeron
- **conducir:** conduje, condujiste, condujo, condujimos, condujisteis, condujeron
- **creer:** creí, creíste, creyó, creímos, creísteis, creyeron
- **dar:** di, diste, dio, dimos, disteis, dieron
- **decir:** dije, dijiste, dijo, dijimos, dijisteis, dijeron
- **detener:** detuve, detuviste, detuvo, detuvimos, detuvisteis, detuvieron
- **estar:** estuve, estuviste, estuvo, estuvimos, estuvisteis, estuvieron
- **haber:** hube, hubiste, hubo, hubimos, hubisteis, hubieron
- **hacer:** hice, hiciste, hizo, hicimos, hicisteis, hicieron
- **ir:** fui, fuiste, fue, fuimos, fuisteis, fueron
- **leer:** leí, leíste, leyó, leímos, leísteis, leyeron
- **poder:** pude, pudiste, pudo, pudimos, pudisteis, pudieron
- **poner:** puse, pusiste, puso, pusimos, pusisteis, pusieron
- **querer:** quise, quisiste, quiso, quisimos, quisisteis, quisieron
- **reír:** reí, reíste, rió, reímos, reísteis, rieron
- **saber:** supe, supiste, supo, supimos, supisteis, supieron
- **ser:** fui, fuiste, fue, fuimos, fuisteis, fueron
- **tener:** tuve, tuviste, tuvo, tuvimos, tuvisteis, tuvieron

- **traer:** traje, trajiste, trajo, trajimos, trajisteis, trajeron
- **traducir:** traduje, tradujiste, tradujo, tradujimos, tradujisteis, tradujeron
- **venir:** vine, viniste, vino, vinimos, vinisteis, vinieron
- **ver:** vi, viste, vio, vimos, visteis, vieron

Past Participles

- **abrir** (to open): abierto
- **caer** (to fall): caído
- **cubrir** (to cover): cubierto
- **decir** (to say): dicho
- **descubrir** (to discover): descubierto
- **deshacer** (to undo): deshecho
- **devolver** (to return, give back): devuelto
- **envolver** (to wrap up): envuelto
- **escribir** (to write): escrito
- **imponer** (to impose): impuesto
- **imprimir** (to print): impreso
- **ir** (to go): ido
- **leer** (to read): leído
- **morir** (to die): muerto
- **oír** (to hear): oído
- **poner** (to put, place): puesto
- **rehacer** (to redo, remake): rehecho
- **reír** (to laugh): reído
- **resolver** (to resolve, solve): resuelto
- **romper** (to break): roto
- **traer** (to bring): traído
- **ver** (to see): visto
- **volver** (to return): vuelto

> *Examples:*
> - The door is open.
>   **La puerta está abierta.**
> - The differences are seen.
>   **Las diferencias están vistas.**

Future & Conditional

■ The following 12 verbs change the stems for both the future and the conditional tenses:
   ◆ **caber:** cabr
   ◆ **decir:** dir
   ◆ **haber:** habr
   ◆ **hacer:** har
   ◆ **poder:** podr
   ◆ **poner:** pondr
   ◆ **querer:** querr
   ◆ **saber:** sabr
   ◆ **salir:** saldr
   ◆ **tener:** tendr
   ◆ **valer:** valdr
   ◆ **venir:** vendr

Present Subjunctive

■ **dar:** dé, dés, demos, deis, den
■ **estar:** esté, estés, esté, estemos, estéis, estén
■ **haber:** haya, hayas, haya, hayamos, hayáis, hayan
■ **ir:** vaya, vayas, vaya, vayamos, vayáis, vayan
■ **saber:** sepa, sepas, sepa, sepamos, sepáis, sepan
■ **ser:** sea, seas, sea, seamos, seáis, sean

Imperative

- **decir:** di
- **hacer:** haz
- **ir:** ve
- **poner:** pon
- **salir:** sal
- **tener:** ten
- **valer:** vale
- **venir:** ven

Auxiliary Verb Used to Form Perfect Tenses

-er ending: **haber** = to have
Pres. Part.: **habiendo**; Past Part.: **habido**

- **Present**   he, has, ha, hemos, habéis, han
- **Imperfect** había, habías, había, habíamos, habíais, habían
- **Preterit**   hube, hubiste, hubo, hubimos, hubisteis, hubieron
- **Future**   habré, habrás, habrá, habremos, habréis, habrán
- **Conditional** habría, habrías, habría, habríamos, habríais, habrían
- **Pres. Subj.** haya, hayas, haya, hayamos, hayáis, hayan
- **Past Subj.** hubiera, hubieras, hubiera, hubiéramos, hubierais, hubieran

Imperfect Tense

■ **ir:** iba, ibas, iba, íbamos, ibais, iban
■ **ser:** era, eras, era, éramos, erais, eran
■ **ver:** veía, veías, veía, veíamos, veíais, veían

Orthographic (Spelling) Changes

■ **acercarse:** me acerqué
■ **almorzar:** almorcé
■ **buscar:** busqué
■ **comenzar:** comencé
■ **gozar:** gocé
■ **llegar:** llegué
■ **pagar:** pagué
■ **sacar:** saqué

Stem-Changing Verbs

■ Change their form in the present tense in all forms *except the first- and second-person plural (nosotros, nosotras, vosotros and vosotras)*. To conjugate, drop the ending and change the "e" of the last syllable to "ie;" the "o" of the last syllable to "ue;" or the "e" to "i."

■ Verbs which change from "e" to "ie."
   ◆ Include the following:
   pensar (to think); **querer** (to want, like, love); **calentar** (to heat); **cerrar** (to close); **comenzar** (to begin); **despertar** (to awaken); **empezar** (to begin); **entender** (to understand); **mentir** (to lie, not tell the truth); **negar** (to deny); **perder** (to lose); **preferir** (to prefer); **sentar** (to seat); **sentir** (to regret, feel).

◆ Conjugations in the present tense include **pienso, piensas, piensa, pensamos, penséis and piensan.**

> *Examples:*
> - I think about freedom.
>   **Yo pienso en la libertad.**
> - I'm sorry. OR I regret it.
>   **Lo siento.**

■ Verbs which change from "o" to "ue."
   ◆ Include the following:
   acostarse (to lie down); **contar** (to count); **poder** (to be able); **costar** (to cost); **dormir** (to sleep); **encontrar** (to find, meet); **jugar** (to play); **morir** (to die); **mostrar** (to show); **volar** (to fly); **volver** (to return).
   ◆ Conjugations in the present tense include **cuento, cuentas, cuenta, contamos, contáis, and cuentan.**

> *Examples:*
> - You count the sheep.
>   **Tú cuentas las ovejas.**

■ Verbs which change from "e" to "i."
   ◆ Include the following:
   conseguir (to obtain); **corregir** (to correct); **elegir** (to elect, choose); **impedir** (to prevent); **pedir** (to request, ask for); **repetir** (to repeat); **seguir** (to follow); **servir** (to serve); **vestir** (to dress).

> *Examples:*
> - She is asking for cold water.
>   **Ella pide agua fría.**
> - They continue running.
>   **Siguen corriendo.**

◆ In the case of **pedir**, conjugations in the present tense include **pido, pides, pide, pedimos, pédis,** and **piden.**

■ **Jugar** (to play) has rules of its own, as a stem-changing verb. Its "u" changes to "ue," as follows: **juego, juegas, juega, jugamos, jugáis** and **juegan.**

> *Examples:*
> - He plays tennis.
>   **El juega al tenis.**

■ **Oler** (to smell) also has an unusual change. Its "o" changes to "hue," as follows: **huelo, hueles, huele, olemos, oléis,** and **huelen.**

> *Examples:*
> - It doesn't smell good.
>   **No huele bien.**

Important Irregular Verbs
■ **Gustar**
   ◆ Definition
     • To be pleasing to someone
     • Used mostly in the third-person singular and plural; conveys the idea of liking something
   ◆ Sentence structure: indirect object pronoun, verb, article and noun or infinitive.

> *Examples:*
> - I like this book.
>   **Me gusta este libro.**
> - Do you like cold milk?
>   **¿Te gusta la leche fría?**
> - We liked to sing.
>   **Nos gustaba cantar.**

■ Haber

- ◆ Root for the phrases that communicate the ideas of "there is" and "there are."
- ◆ Serves as a helping verb for the perfect tenses.
- ◆ In the **"hay"** conjugation, communicates the idea of "there is" and "there are."

Examples:
- It is very sunny. *OR* There is much sun.
  Hay mucho sol.
- There are many clouds in the sky.
  Hay muchas nubes en el cielo.
- There is no doubt.
  No hay duda.

- ◆ Related uses: **Había** (There was/were); **hubo** (there was/were/used to be); **habrá** (there will be); **ha habido** (there has/have been); **haya** (may there be); **puede haber** (there could be); **debe haber** (there must be); **puede haber** (there can be); **podía haber** or **podría haber** (there could be); **había habido** (there had been).

Examples:
- The moon was shining brilliantly that night.
  OR There was brilliant moonlight that night.
  Había una luna brillante esa noche.
  There was no problem.
  No había problema.
  Let there be light.
  Que haya luz.

- ◆ Use the **"hay"** or **"había"** forms with the infinitive of a verb to communicate a general requirement: **Hay que esperar.** (One must wait.); **No había que vender nada.** (It wasn't necessary to sell anything.); **Habrá que tener cuidado.** (It will be necessary to be careful.)

◆ Like the phrase **"De nada,"** **"no hay de qué"** means "you're welcome." It is actually short for **"No hay de qué dar gracias."** ("No thanks are necessary.")

■ **Hacer**
   ◆ Communicates the ideas of "to make" and "to do."
   ◆ Used, in the third-person singular, to express various ideas about weather: **Hace sol.** (It is sunny.); **Hacía mucho fresco.** (It was very cool.); **Hará buen tiempo.** (There will be good weather.); **Hacía muchsimo viento.** (It was extremely windy.); **Hará mucho calor.** (It will be very hot.); **¿Qué tiempo hace?** (What kind of weather is it?)
   ◆ Used to indicate the idea of past time, in the sense of "ago" or "since:" **Comenzó hace muchos años.** (It began many years ago.); **Hace muchos meses pasaron por aquí.** (They passed by here many months ago.)

■ **Ir**
   ◆ To go
   ◆ To communicate a sense of future intent: **Yo voy a rezar.** (I'm going to pray.); **Nosotros vamos a triunfar.** (We are going to triumph.)

■ **Poder**
   ◆ Communicates the idea of ability.
   ◆ It is a stem-changing verb, going from "o" to "ue."

Examples:
- You can swim.
  Tú puedes nadar.
- She will be able to walk.
  Ella podrá caminar.
- Might you be able to come?
  ¿Podrían Uds. venir?

■ **Ser/Estar**
  ◆ **Uses of "ser":**
   • Describes permanent characteristics of a person, place, object, or animal: **Miguel es alto, y los otros muchachos son bajos.** (Miguel is tall, and the other boys are short.); **El hielo es frío.** (Ice is cold.)
   • Denotes origin, material, or ownership when followed by the preposition "de": **Somos de Wyoming.** (We are from Wyoming.)
   • Tells the time and the date: **Es el tres de marzo, y son las cuatro de la tarde.** (It's the third of March, and it's four in the afternoon.)
   • Forms the passive voice: **La fonografía fue inventada por Thomas Edison.** (The phonograph was invented by Thomas Edison.)
  ◆ **Uses of estar:**
   • Expresses location: **Estamos en el jardín.** (We are in the garden.)
   • Expresses a condition: **Ella está muy contenta.** (She is very happy.); **Está nublado.** (It is cloudy.) **Está despejado.** (It is clear.)
   • Forms the progressive tenses: **Yo estaba escuchando durante el día.** (I was listening during the day.); **Alfredo está ayudando.** (Alfredo is helping.)
■ **Tener**
  ◆ Expresses possession: **Diana tiene una bicicleta roja.** (Diana has a red bicycle.)
  ◆ Expresses a broad range of conditions, including the following:
   • **Tener calor** (to be or feel warm): **Isabel tiene calor.** (Isabel is warm. OR Isabel feels very warm.)

- **Tener cuidado** (to be careful): **Hay que tener cuidado.** (One must be careful.)
- **Tener deseos** (to be eager, to wish very much): **Los muchachos tienen muchos deseos de participar.** (The children are eager to participate.)
- **Tener éxito** (to be successful): **Que tengas mucho éxito.** (May you have much success.)
- **Tener frío** (to be or feel cold): **Juan tiene mucho frío.** (Juan is very cold. OR Juan feels very cold.); **Tengo frío.** (I am cold. OR I feel cold.)
- **Tener ganas** (to feel like, be in the mood for): **Tengo ganas de bailar.** (I feel like dancing.)
- **Tener hambre** (to be hungry): **Tuve muchísima hambre.** (I was extremely hungry.)
- **Tener la culpa** (to be at fault): **¿Crees que yo tenga la culpa?** (Do you think it might be my fault?)
- **Tener miedo** (to be afraid): **Ellos tienen mucho miedo.** (They are very afraid.)
- **Tener prisa** (to be in a hurry): **No tuvimos prisa.** (We were not in a hurry.)
- **Tener razón** (to be right): **Es posible que Uds.** tengan razón. (It's possible that you are right.)
- **Tener sed** (to be thirsty): **¿Tienen ellos mucha sed?** (Are they very thirsty?)
- **Tener sueño** (to be sleepy): **Tendremos mucho sueño.** (We will be very sleepy.)
- **Tener suerte** (to be lucky, fortunate): **Que José tenga suerte.** (May José be lucky.)
- **Tener vergüenza** (to be ashamed): **Ellos no tienen vergüenza.** (They have no shame.)

◆ Expresses a person's age: **Tengo diecinueve años.** (I am 19 years old).; **Mi bisabuela tiene noventa años.** (My great-grandmother is 90 years old.); **¿Cuántos años tiene Ud.?** (How old are you?)

◆ Expresses concern about a strange situation or odd behavior: **¿Qué tiene Ud.?** (What's wrong with you?); **¿Qué tienen ellos?** (What is the matter with them?)

◆ Can be matched with **que** and the infinitive of a verb in order to communicate the idea of having to do something: **Ella tiene que ayudar.** (She has to help.); **No tendremos que esperar.** (We won't have to wait.)

Tense, Form & Usage

Indicative Mood

Present Tense

■ **Usage**
- ◆ Describe events occurring now or that occur regularly.
- ◆ Also used to express a condition in the near future.

Present	-ar (hablar)	-er (comer)	-ir (escribir)
Yo	habl + o	com + o	escrib + o
Tú	habl + as	com + es	escrib + es
El	habl + a	com + e	escrib + e
Ella	habl + a	com + e	escrib + e
Usted	habl + a	com + e	escrib + e
Nosotros	habl + amos	com + emos	escrib + imos
Vosotros	habl + áis	com + éis	escrib + ís
Ellas	habl + an	com + en	escrib + en
Ellos	habl + an	com + en	escrib + en
Ustedes	habl + an	com + en	escrib + en

Imperfect

■ **Usage**
- ◆ Describes what was happening or used to happen in the past.
- ◆ It is used for background; descriptions of persons or things as well as for habitual or customary actions.

- ◆ The expressions usually associated with the imperfect are: **siempre, a menudo, todos los días, todas las semanas, todos los años, frecuentemente,** etc.
- ◆ **Yo hablaba** is normally translated as "I used to speak" or "I was speaking."

	-ar (hablar)	-er (comer)	-ir (escribir)
Yo	habl + aba	com + ía	escrib + ía
Tú	habl + abas	com + ías	escrib + ías
El	habl + aba	com + ía	escrib + ía
Ella	habl + aba	com + ía	escrib + ía
Usted	habl + aba	com + ía	escrib + ía
Nosotros	habl + ábamos	com + íamos	escrib + íamos
Vosotros	habl + abais	com + íais	escrib + íais
Ellas	habl + aban	com + ían	escrib + ían
Ellos	habl + aban	com + ían	escrib + ían
Ustedes	habl + aban	com + ían	escrib + ían

Preterit

■ Usage

- ◆ Emphasizes beginning, end or completeness of an action or state within a certain period of time in the past.
- ◆ Words normally associated with the preterite: **ayer, el año pasado, la semana pasada, anoche,** etc.
- ◆ **Yo hablé** is usually translated as "I spoke."

	-ar (hablar)	-er (comer)	-ir (escribir)
Yo	habl + é	com + í	escrib + í
Tú	habl + aste	com + iste	escrib + iste
El	habl + ó	com + ió	escrib + ió
Ella	habl + ó	com + ió	escrib + ió
Usted	habl + ó	com + ió	escrib + ió
Nosotros	habl + amos	com + imos	escrib + imos
Vosotros	habl + asteis	com + isteis	escrib + isteis
Ellos/Ellas	habl + aron	com + ieron	escrib + ieron
Ustedes	habl + aron	com + ieron	escrib + ieron

NOTES
Imperfect vs. Preterit
In a narration, the preterit is used to tell the story or relate past events, while the imperfect is used to describe the background or set the stage for the story.

Future
■ **Usage**
- ◆ Describes events that will occur in the future.
- ◆ Also expresses uncertainty or speculation in the present.

■ **Formation**
- ◆ Adding the endings of the present tense of the auxiliary verb **haber** to the infinitive.
- ◆ Written accents occur in all persons except the first person plural.

	-ar (hablar)	-er (comer)	-ir (escribir)
Yo	hablar + é	comer + é	escribir + é
Tú	hablar + ás	comer + ás	escribir + ás
El	hablar + á	comer + á	escribir + á
Ella	hablar + á	comer + á	escribir + á
Usted	hablar + á	comer + á	escribir + á
Nosotros	hablar + emos	comer + emos	escribir + emos
Vosotros	hablar + éis	comer + éis	escribir + éis
Ellos/Ellas	hablar + án	comer + án	excribir + án
Ustedes	hablar + án	comer + án	excribir + án

> **NOTES**
> **Future & Conditional**
> Both use the infinitive form of the verb as the stem before adding the endings of future and conditional.

Conditional
■ Formation
◆ Adding the imperfect endings of the second and third conjugation to the infinitive.

	-ar (hablar)	-er (comer)	-ir (escribir)
Yo	hablar + ía	comer + ía	escribir + ía
Tú	hablar + ías	comer + ías	escribir + ías
El	hablar + ía	comer + ía	escribir + ía
Ella	hablar + ía	comer + ía	escribir + ía
Usted	hablar + ía	comer + ía	escribir + ía
Nosotros	hablar + íamos	comer + íamos	escribir + íamos
Vosotros	hablar + íais	comer + íais	escribir + íais
Ellos	hablar + ían	comer + ían	escribir + ían
Ellas	hablar + ían	comer + ían	escribir + ían
Ustedes	hablar + ían	comer + ían	escribir + ían

■ Usage
◆ Expresses uncertainty, feelings, desires, and hypothetical situations. **Saldría a esa hora.** (He/she probably left at that time.)
◆ It is used to make a request or a polite statement: **¿Podría usted venir conmigo?** (Could you come with me?)

Subjunctive Mood
Present Subjunctive
■ Formation
◆ Drop **"o"** from the first person singular form of the present indicative **(hablo, pienso, traigo *become* habl, piens, traig)** and add the subjunctive endings.

	-ar (hablar)	-er (comer)	-ir (escribir)
Yo	habl + e	com + a	escrib + a
Tú	habl + es	com + as	escrib + as
El	habl + e	com + a	escrib + a
Ella	habl + e	com + a	escrib + a
Usted	habl + e	com + a	escrib + a
Nosotros	habl + emos	com + amos	escrib + amos
Vosotros	habl + éis	com + áis	escrib + áis
Ellos	habl + en	com + an	escrib + an
Ellas	habl + en	com + an	escrib + an
Ustedes	habl + en	com + an	escrib + an

Imperfect Subjunctive
■ **Formation**
   ◆ Take the third person plural form of the preterite tense, drop the **ron** ending and add the imperfect subjunctive endings.

	-ar (hablar)	-er (comer)	-ir (escribir)
Yo	habla + ra	comie + ra	escribie + ra
Tú	habla + ras	comie + ras	escribie + ras
El	habla + ra	comie + ra	escribie + ra
Ella	habla + ra	comie + ra	escribie + ra
Usted	habla + ra	comie + ra	escribie + ra
Nosotros	hablá + ramos	comié + ramos	escribié + ramos
Vosotros	habla + rais	comie + rais	escribie + rais
Ellos	habla + ran	comie + ran	escribie + ran
Ellas	habla + ran	comie + ran	escribie + ran
Ustedes	habla + ran	comie + ran	escribie + ran

Usage

■ Verbs and phrases

◆ After a verb or impersonal phrase that expresses a wish, desire, preference, suggestion or request: **Quiero que tú estudies.** (I want you to study.)

◆ After a verb or expression that expresses doubt, fear, joy, hope, sorrow or some other emotion: **Quizás ella venga.** (Perhaps she will come.)

◆ After certain impersonal expressions that show necessity, doubt, regret, possibility: **Es necesario.** (It's necessary.) **Es posible.** (It's possible.) **Es una lástima.** (It's a shame.)

■ Conjunctions

◆ After conjunctions denoting purpose, provision or exception: **para que** (in order that), **a fin de que** (so that), **con tal de que** (provided that), **en caso (de) que** (in case), **a menos que** (unless), **sin que** (without): **Lo dijo para que ellos lo supieran.** (She/He said it so that they would know it.)

◆ After certain conjunctions of time if the action has not occurred, such as **mientras que, cuando, en cuanto, después de, hasta que, tan pronto como**: *Comeremos tan pronto como mis padres lleguen.* (We will eat as soon as my parents arrive.)

■ Clauses

◆ In adjectival (or relative) clauses when antecedent (noun or pronoun) in main clause is indefinite or nonexistent: **Busco un estudiante que hable japonés.** (I am looking for a student who speaks Japanese.)

Subjunctive Sequence of Tenses

■ When the use of the subjunctive is required:

◆ If the verb in the main clause is in the present, future or present perfect indicative, or the imperative, then the present or present perfect subjunctive is used in the dependent clause: **Queremos que tú asistas a la escuela.** (We want you to attend school.); **Empieza a preparar la cena para que ellas puedan salir temprano.** (Start preparing dinner so that they may go out early.)

◆ If the verb in the main clause is in the imperfect indicative, preterite, conditional, or pluperfect indicative, then the imperfect or pluperfect subjunctive is used in the dependent clause. **Queríamos que tú asistieras a la escuela.** (We wanted you to attend school.); **Empecé a preparar la cena para que ellas pudieran salir temprano.** (I began to prepare dinner so that they might leave early.)

Imperative Mood

■ Used to express a command.

◆ The imperative is used in the following persons: **tú, nosotros(as), vosotros(as), usted** and **ustedes,** but the subject pronoun is not expressed.

◆ The affirmative command forms for **nosotros(as), vosotros(as), usted** and **ustedes,** as well as all negative commands, are derived from the present subjunctive tense: **Llámeme mañana** (call me tomorrow.) **Estudiemos ahora.** (Let's study now.)

◆ The **tú** form affirmative is the same as the third person singular of the present tense: **habla, come,** and **escribe.**

Compound Tenses

Perfect Tenses

◆ The different compound tenses are formed by
using the auxiliary verb **haber** in the present,
imperfect, future and conditional of the
indicative mood and the present and imperfect
of the subjunctive with the past participles of the
main verb.

◆ The present perfect of **hablar** consists of the
present tense of **haber** plus the past participle of
hablar: *Yo he hablado.* (I have spoken.)

◆ The past perfect of **hablar** consists of the
imperfect of **haber** plus the past participle of
hablar: *Yo había hablado.* (I had spoken.)

◆ The future perfect of **hablar** consists of the
future of **haber** plus the past participle of
hablar: *Yo habré hablado.* (I will have spoken.)

◆ The conditional perfect of **hablar** consists of the
conditional of haber plus the past participle of
hablar: *Yo habría hablado.* (I would have spoken.)

◆ The present perfect subjunctive of **hablar**
consists of the present subjunctive of **haber** plus
the past participle of **hablar**: *Que yo haya
hablado.* (I may have spoken.)

◆ The past perfect subjunctive of **hablar** consists of the imperfect subjunctive of **haber** plus the past participle of **hablar:** *Yo hubiera hablado.* (I might have spoken.)

Progressive Tenses
■ **Formation**
◆ The progressive tenses are formed by the present or imperfect tense of the verb **estar** and the present participle of the main conjugated verb.
◆ Thus the present progressive is: *Yo estoy hablando.* (I am speaking.) And the past progressive is: *Yo estaba hablando.* (I was speaking.)

■ **Usage**
◆ The progressive tenses are limited in their use to an action that is happening right at that moment: **Estoy almorzando.** (I am [now] eating lunch.) For an action that is not taking place yet, the present tense or the near future is used: **Voy a almorzar.** (I'm going to eat lunch.); **Almuerzo al mediodia.** (I eat lunch at noon.)
◆ The following verbs are rarely used in the present progressive: **ir, venir, estar,** and **ser.**

Present Participle
■ Equivalent to the English **-ing** form
■ **Formation**
◆ By dropping the **ar** from **-ar** verbs and adding **ando** and the **er** or **ir** from **-er** and **-ir** verbs and adding **iendo** to the stem: **hablar - hablando, comer - comiendo, escribir - escribiendo.**

Examples:
Irregular Present Participles
- **caer:** cayendo
- **creer:** creyendo
- **decir:** diciendo
- **dormir:** durmiendo
- **ir:** yendo
- **leer:** leyendo
- **mentir:** mintiendo
- **morir:** muriendo
- **oír:** oyendo
- **pedir:** pidiendo
- **poder:** pudiendo
- **preferir:** prefiriendo
- **reír:** riendo
- **seguir:** siguiendo
- **sentir:** sintiendo
- **ser:** siendo
- **servir:** sirviendo
- **traer:** trayendo
- **venir:** viniendo

Past Participle

■ Past participle of regular verbs are formed:
- ◆ By dropping the infinitive ending **ar** of the first conjugation and adding **ado: caminar - caminado.**
- ◆ In the second and third conjugations, by replacing the endings **er** and **ir** with **ido: entender - entendido; recibir - recibido.**

Examples:
Irregular Past Participles
- **abrir:** abierto
- **caer:** caído
- **creer:** creído
- **cubrir:** cubierto
- **decir:** dicho
- **describir:** descrito
- **escribir:** escrito
- **freír:** frito
- **hacer:** hecho
- **ir:** ido
- **leer:** leído
- **morir:** muerto
- **oír:** oído
- **poner:** puesto
- **reír:** reído
- **romper:** roto
- **ser:** sido
- **traer:** traído
- **ver:** visto
- **volver:** vuelto

Reflexive Verbs

NOTES
With reflexive verbs, the subject receives the action of the verb. (Usually, the subject **performs** the action.)

■ **Formation**
◆ By using the reflexive pronouns in front of the conjugated verb: **Mi hijo se levanta, se baña y se viste.** (My son gets up, takes a bath and gets dressed.)

■ They describe some actions, such as hygiene, which one performs on oneself, and are distinguished by the **"se"** at the end of the infinitive.

Examples:
- "to brush one's teeth"
  Cepillarse los dientes
- "to put on" (often in the sense of putting on clothing)
  Ponerse
- "to lie down"
  Acostarse
- "to get married"
  Casarse
- "to wash oneself"
  Lavarse
- "to get up"
  Levantarse
- "to put on makeup"
  Maquillarse
- "to sit down"
  Sentarse
- "to dress oneself"
  Vestirse

■ Some verbs assume a different meaning when they become reflexive.

◆ Among them are **irse** (to go away) and **dormirse** (to fall asleep), as compared to **ir** (to go) and **dormir** (to sleep):

Me voy ahora. (I'm going away now.); **¿Te duermes?** (Are you falling asleep?)

Examples:

Common Reflexive Verbs:
- ◆ **aburrirse**
- ◆ **acostarse**
- ◆ **afeitarse**
- ◆ **bañarse**
- ◆ **caerse**
- ◆ **callarse**
- ◆ **cansarse**
- ◆ **cepillarse**
- ◆ **despedirse**
- ◆ **despertarse**
- ◆ **divertirse**
- ◆ **enojarse**
- ◆ **equivocarse**
- ◆ **irse**
- ◆ **levantarse**
- ◆ **peinarse**
- ◆ **ponerse**
- ◆ **prepararse**
- ◆ **quitarse**
- ◆ **sentirse**

19 Verb Essentials

■ **Infinitives**
*The verb in its most basic form, such as **hablar** (to speak), **comer** (to eat) and **vivir** (to live).*

♦ The **stem,** or **radical:** The first portion of the verb, such as **habl-, com-,** and **viv-**

♦ **Infinitive ending:** The last two letters in the verb, such as **–ar, -er,** and **–ir**

♦ Verbs are **usually** conjugated by removing the infinitive ending and applying a new ending, corresponding to a certain set of rules.

■ **English/Spanish Comparison**
♦ In English, most verbs differ only between the third-person singular and the other tenses.

♦ Thus, the options for the simple present tense in English for the verb "speak" are *I speak, you speak, he speaks, she speaks, they speak* and *we speak. "Speak"* and *"speaks" are the only options in that tense.*

♦ Spanish, however, has *six* distinct possible endings for that verb (hablar) in the present tense.

■ **In Spanish, verbs have six conjugations in each tense – one for each subject pronoun.** To use the verb **hablar** in the simple present tense, take the stem – **habl** – and attach an ending according to the following guidelines:

- ◆ **Yo:** (first-person, singular pronoun) **habl + o** – I speak
- ◆ **Tú:** (second-person, singular familiar pronoun) **habl + as** – you speak
- ◆ **Usted:** (second-person, singular formal pronoun, often abbreviated as Ud.) **habl + a** – you speak
- ◆ **El:** (third-person, singular, male pronoun) **habl + a** – he speaks
- ◆ **Ella:** (third-person, singular, female pronoun) **habl + a** – she speaks
- ◆ **Nosotros:** (first-person, plural, male or mixed-gender pronoun) **habl + amos** – we speak
- ◆ **Nosotras:** (first-person, plural, female pronoun) **habl + amos** – we speak
- ◆ **Vosotros:** (second-person, plural, familiar, male or mixed-gender pronoun) **habl + áis** – you speak
- ◆ **Vosotras:** (second-person, plural, familiar, female pronoun) **habl + áis** – you speak

NOTES
The "vosotros" and "vosotras" forms are primarily used in Spain, and are less common in other Spanish-speaking countries. Except for Spaniards, most Spanish speakers use the "**ustedes**" form, as described below.

- ◆ **Ustedes:** (second-person, plural formal pronoun, often abbreviated as Uds.) **habl + an** – you speak
- ◆ **Ellos:** (third-person, plural, male or mixed-gender pronoun) **habl + an** – they speak
- ◆ **Ellas:** (third-person, plural, female pronoun) **habl + an** – they speak

Useful & Essential Verbs

* = irregular verb
** = stem-changing verb
*** = irregular, stem-changing

A

abandonar: to abandon
abatir: to overthrow
abolir*: to abolish
abrazar*: to hug, embrace
abrir*: to open
aceptar: to accept
acostar**: to put to bed
acostumbrar: to accustom
adaptar: to adapt, adjust, fit
admitir: to admit
adorar: to worship, adore
alegrar: to make happy, cheer up
almorzar***: to have lunch
amar: to love
andar*: to walk
anticipar: to anticipate
aplaudir: to applaud
aplicar: to apply
aprender: to learn
asistir: to attend
ayudar: to help

B

bailar: to dance
bajar: to descend, lower
bastar: to be enough, suffice
beber: to drink
besar: to kiss

C

caer*: to fall
calentar**: to heat
cambiar: to change
caminar: to walk
cansar: to wear out, tire
casar: to marry
cenar: to eat supper
cerrar**: to close
cocinar: to cook
comenzar***: to commence, begin
comer: to eat
compartir: to share
comprar: to buy
comprender: to understand
comunicar*: to communicate
confiar*: to have trust, be trusting
conseguir**: to get, obtain
construir*: to build
contar**: to count
contestar: to answer
convertir**: to convert
corregir***: to correct
correr: to run
costar**: to cost
creer*: to believe
cruzar: to cross
cubrir*: to cover
cuidarse: to take care of oneself
cumplir: to complete

D

dar*: to give
deber: to owe, have a moral obligation
decidir: to decide
decir*: to say, tell
dejar: to allow, permit, let, leave
desayunar: to have breakfast
desear: to want
describir*: to describe
descubrir*: to discover
deshacer*: to undo, destroy
destruir: to destroy
devolver***: to refund, give back
disculpar: to forgive
discutir: to discuss, argue
divertir**: to amuse
divorciar: to divorce
doblar: to bend, double, fold
dormir***: to sleep
dudar: to doubt

E

elegir***: to elect, choose
empezar**: to begin
encontrar**: to encounter, find
enojar: to anger
entender**: to understand
entrar: to enter
envolver***: to wrap up
esconder: to hide
escribir*: to write
escuchar: to listen

esperar: to wait, hope
estar*: to be
estudiar: to study
existir: to exist
explicar*: to explain
extrañar: to miss [someone]

F
fumar: to smoke
funcionar: to function

G
gastar: to spend [money]
golpear: to hit, strike
guiar*: to guide
gustar: to be pleasing [to someone or something]

H
haber*: to have, as a helping verb to form compound
          tenses
hablar: to speak
hacer*: to do, make
huir*: to flee

I
impedir**: to prevent
imponer*: to impose
imprimir*: to print
interrumpir*: to interrupt
invitar: to invite
ir*: to go

J
jugar**: to play [a sport or game]
jurar: to swear, take an oath

L
leer*: to read
levantar: to raise
llamar: to call
llegar*: to arrive
llenar: to fill
llevar: to carry, wear

M
mandar: to send
matar: to kill
mentir**: to tell a lie
meter: to put [in]
mirar: to look
morir***: to die
mostrar**: to show
mudarse: to change one's place of residence, change one's clothes, move

N
nacer*: to be born
nadar: to swim
necesitar: to need
negar**: to deny

O

ocurrir: to occur
oír*: to hear
oler***: to smell, scent
olvidar: to forget
oponer*: to oppose
orar: to pray

P

pagar*: to pay
parar: to stop
parecer*: to appear, look, seem
pasar: to happen, pass [by]
pedir***: to request
pensar**: to think
perder**: to lose
perdonar: to pardon
platicar*: to chat, converse
poder***: to be able
poner*: to put
poseer*: to possess, own
predicar*: to preach
preferir**: to prefer
preparar: to prepare
preguntar: to ask
probar**: to prove, try
prometer: to promise
proveer*: to provide

Q

quedar: to remain, stay
quejarse: to complain, grumble
querer***: to want
quitar: to take off [clothing]

R

recibir: to receive
reconocer*: to recognize, acknowledge
recordar**: to remember, recollect
regalar: to give [as a gift]
registrar: to register, record
regresar: to return
rehacer*: to redo, remake
reír*: to laugh
repetir**: to repeat
resolver**: to resolve
rezar*: to pray
romper*: to break

S

saber*: to know
sacar*: to get, take out
salir*: to leave
saludar: to greet, say hello to
seguir**: to continue
sentir**: to feel, regret
separar: to separate, detach
ser*: to be
servir**: to serve
sonreír*: to smile
sorprender: to surprise
subir: to ascend, climb
sufrir: to suffer

T

temer: to fear
tener***: to have
tocar*: to touch, to play [music or a musical instrument]
tomar: to take, drink
tostar**: to toast
trabajar: to work
traer*: to bring
tratar: to try

U

unir: to unite
usar: to use

V

vender: to sell
venir***: to come
ver*: to see
vestirse**: to clothe oneself, dress oneself
viajar: to travel
visitar: to visit
vivir: to live
volar***: to fly
volver***: to return

Measurements

20

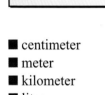
- centimeter   **el centímetro** (0.39 in.)
- meter   **el metro** (3.28 feet)
- kilometer   **el kilómetro** (0.621 mile)
- liter   **el litro** (1.75 pints)
- gram   **el gramo** (0.0352 oz.)
- kilogram   **el kilo (gramo)** (2.20 lbs.)

Clothes

21

NOTES
Clothes = **La Ropa**

Examples:
- "It looks good on you!"
  "¡Le queda/sienta bien!"

- "What is your size?"
  "¿Cuál es su talla?"

For plurals, add **"s"** unless the word ends in a consonant, in which case add **"es."**

■ (hand)bag	**la cartera**
■ bathing (swim) suit	**el traje de baño**
■ belt	**el cinturón**
■ blouse	**la blusa**
■ boots	**las botas**
■ bra	**el sostén**
■ cap	**la gorra**
■ cheap	**barato/a**
■ coat	**el abrigo**
■ cotton	**algodón**
■ dress	**el vestido**

■ expensive	**caro/a**
■ hat	**el sombrero**
■ jacket	**la chaqueta**
■ jeans	**los vaqueros**
■ lace	**la puntilla**
■ leather	**el cuero**
■ nightgown	**el camisón**
■ pants	**los pantalones**
■ pantyhose	**las medias de nylon**
■ parka	**el anorak**
■ pajamas	**el pijama**
■ raincoat	**el impermeable**
■ rubber boots	**los zapatos de goma**
■ sandal	**la sandalia**
■ scarf	**la bufanda**
■ shirt	**la camisa**
■ shoe	**el zapato**
■ shorts	**los pantalones cortos**
■ silk	**la seda**
■ size	**el talla**
■ skirt	**la falda**
■ sleeve	**la manga**
■ slip	**la enagua**
■ sock	**el calcetín**
■ suit	**el traje**
■ sweater	**el suéter**
■ tennis shoes	**los zapatos de tenis**
■ T-shirt	**la camiseta**
■ tie	**la corbata**
■ umbrella	**el paraguas**
■ underwear	**la ropa interior**
■ wallet	**la billetera**
■ wool	**la lana**

Color

NOTES
Color = **El Color**

- beige   **beige**
- black   **negro/a**
- blue   **azul**
- brown   **marrón**
- green   **verde**
- grey   **gris**
- orange   **anaranjado/a**
- pink   **rosado/a**
- purple   **morado/a**
- red   **rojo/a**
- yellow   **amarillo/a**
- white   **blanco/a**
- dark   **oscuro/a**
- light   **claro/a**

23 Bank

Examples:
- to buy
  comprar
- "How much do I owe you?"
  "¿Cuánto yo le debo a usted?"
- "How much is it?"
  "¿Cuánto es?"
- "I would like... please."
  "Me gustaría... por favor."
- "It's expensive!"
  "¡Es caro!"
- to place an order
  hacer un pedido
- to complain
  quejarse
- to cash a check
  cobrar un cheque
- to order
  encargar
- to pay the bill
  pagar la cuenta

For plurals, add "**s**" unless the word ends in a consonant, in which case add "**es**."

Examples:
el dólar, los dólares

■ account	**la cuenta**
■ balance	**el saldo**
■ bank	**el banco**
■ bank account	**la cuenta de banco**
■ bill	**la cuenta**
■ business trip	**el viaje de negocios**
■ calendar	**el calendario**
■ cash	**el efectivo**
■ cash register	**la caja**
■ -to change	**cambiar**
■ -to clear up	**pagar**
■ complaint	**la queja**
■ credit card	**la tarjeta de crédito**
■ customer	**el cliente**
■ customs	**la aduana**
■ customs officer	**el oficial de aduanas**
■ delivery	**la entrega**
■ department store	**el almacén**
■ dollar	**el dólar**
■ -to endorse	**endosar**
■ exchange bureau	**la oficina de cambio**
■ expenses	**los gastos**
■ interest	**el interés**
■ in writing	**por escrito**
■ mailbox	**el buzón**
■ manager	**el gerente**
■ maturity date	**la fecha de vencimiento**
■ money	**el dinero**

■ money order	**el giro postal**
■ order	**el pedido**
■ payee	**el portador**
■ payment	**el pago**
■ percentage	**el porcentaje**
■ personal check	**el cheque personal**
■ phone book	**la guía de teléfonos**
■ P.O. Box	**el apartado de correos**
■ postage	**el franqueo**
■ postage stamp	**el sello**
■ post office	**el correo**
■ price	**el precio**
■ price (net)	**el precio neto**
■ publicity	**la publicidad**
■ rate	**la tasa**
■ receipt	**el recibo**
■ refund	**reembolso**
■ -to refund	**reembolsar**
■ registered mail	**la carta certificada**
■ salary	**el sueldo**
■ sale	**la venta**
■ sales department	**la sección de ventas**
■ -to save money	**ahorrar**
■ savings	**los ahorros**
■ -to sell	**vender**
■ shipment	**el envío**
■ small change	**cambio**
■ spendings	**los gastos**
■ stocks	**las acciones**
■ -to tax	**gravar or tasar**
■ telegram	**el telegrama**
■ teller	**el cajero**
■ terms of delivery	**las condiciones de reparto**

- terms of payment **las condiciones de pago**
- trade **el comercio**
- transfer **la transferencia**
- -to transfer money **transferir dinero**
- transfer slip **la boleta de transferencia**
- traveler's check **los cheques de viajero**
- valid **válido/a**
- value **el valor**
- wallet **la billetera**
- wire **la transferencia cablegráfica**
- -to wire (money) **transferir dinero**
- withdrawal **el retiro**

Greetings

24

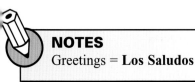
■ hello, Mr.   **hola, señor**
■ hello, Mrs.   **hola, señora**
■ hello, Ms./Miss **hola, señorita**
■ hello/hi   **hola**

Examples:
- "How are you?"
  "¿Cómo está usted?"

- "What is your name?"
  "¿Cómo se llama usted?"

- "My name is..."
  "Me llamo..."

- "I would like to introduce to you..."
  "Yo le presento a usted..."

- "Speak slowly please."
  "Hable lentamente por favor."

■ what?	**¿qué?**
■ fine	**bien**
■ you're welcome	**de nada**
■ not at all	**de ningún modo**
■ delighted	**mucho gusto**
■ very well	**muy bien**
■ not bad	**no está mal**
■ please	**por favor**
■ thank you	**gracias**
■ many thanks	**muchas gracias**
■ good-bye	**adiós**
■ see you soon	**hasta luego**
■ good morning	**buenos días**
■ good afternoon	**buenas tardes**
■ good night	**buenas noches**

NOTES

Travel = **El Viaje**

Directions = **Las Direcciones**

Examples:

- "Be careful!"

  "¡Ten cuidado!"

- "Excuse me, where is...?"

  "¿Perdón, donde es/está...?"

- "Is it far away?"

  "¿Es lejos?"

- "I am lost!"

  "¡Estoy perdido/a!"

For the plural form, add an **"s"** at the end, unless the word ends in a consonant, in which case add **"es."**

Travel

■ address book	**la libreta de direcciones**
■ airport	**el aeropuerto**
■ automobile	**el auto**
■ bicycle	**la bicicleta**
■ boat	**el barco**
■ bus	**el autobús**

◼ camera	**el cámara fotográfica**
◼ cash	**el efectivo**
◼ credit card	**la tarjeta de crédito**
◼ exit	**la salida**
◼ film (a roll)	**la película**
◼ flight	**el vuelo**
◼ guide	**el/la guía**
◼ highway	**la autopista**
◼ map	**el mapa**
◼ money (change)	**la moneda**
◼ money (unit)	**el dinero**
◼ moped	**la bicimoto**
◼ to park	**estacionar**
◼ parking lot	**el estacionamiento**
◼ passerby	**el transeúnte**
◼ passport	**el pasaporte**
◼ plane	**el avión**
◼ police	**la policía**
◼ postcard	**la tarjeta postal**
◼ public	**el público**
◼ reservation	**la reservación**
◼ road	**el camino/la vía**
◼ stop	**el alto**
◼ stoplight	**el semáforo**
◼ subway	**el metro**
◼ sunglasses	**las gafas para el sol**
◼ taxi	**el taxi**
◼ tourism	**el turismo**
◼ tourist	**el/la turista**
◼ town hall	**el ayuntamiento**
◼ traffic circle	**la rotonda**
◼ train	**el tren**
◼ transportation	**el transporte**
◼ train station	**la estación de tren**

■ travel agency	**la agencia de viajes**
■ U-turn	**la vuelta en U**
■ vacations	**las vacaciones**

Directions

■ above, on	**encima/sobre**
■ below, under	**abajo/debajo de**
■ behind	**detrás**
■ in front of	**delante de**
■ between	**entre**
■ facing	**en frente de**
■ next to	**junto a**
■ far	**lejos**
■ near	**cercano/a**
■ at the home of	**en (a) la casa de**
■ at the place of	**en (al) sitio de**
■ there	**allí**
■ here	**acá**
■ outside	**afuera**
■ inside	**adentro**
■ straight ahead	**siga derecho en (a)**
■ at the place of	**en (al) sitio de**
■ there	**allí**
■ here	**acá**
■ (to the) right	**(a la) derecha**
■ (to the) left	**(a la) izquierda**
■ with	**con**
■ without	**sin**
■ north	**el norte**
■ south	**el sur**
■ east	**el este**
■ west	**el oeste**
■ southwest	**el sudoeste**
■ northeast	**el nordeste**

Months, Seasons & Days of the Week

NOTES
Months = **Los Meses**
Seasons = **Las Estaciones**
Days of the Week = **Los Días de la Semana**
Dates = **Las Fechas**

Months

■ January	**enero**
■ February	**febrero**
■ March	**marzo**
■ April	**abril**
■ May	**mayo**
■ June	**junio**
■ July	**julio**
■ August	**agosto**
■ September	**septiembre**
■ October	**octubre**
■ November	**noviembre**
■ December	**diciembre**

Seasons

■ spring	**la primavera**
■ summer	**el verano**
■ fall	**el otoño**
■ winter	**el invierno**

Days of the Week

- Monday   **lunes**
- Tuesday   **martes**
- Wednesday   **miércoles**
- Thursday   **jueves**
- Friday   **viernes**
- Saturday   **sábado**
- Sunday   **domingo**
- weekend   **fin de semana**

Examples:
- "What day is it?"
  "¿Qué día es hoy?"

- "Today is July 14, 2006."
  "Hoy es el catorce de julio de 2006."

27

Time/When

NOTES
Time = **Las Horas**
When = **Cuándo**

Examples:
- "What time is it?"
  "¿Qué hora es?"

- "It is a quarter of 2."
  "Son las dos menos cuarto."

Time

■ 1 A.M.	**la una A.M.**
■ 1:05	**la una y cinco**
■ 2:10	**las dos y diez**
■ 3:15	**las tres y cuarto**
■ 4:30	**las cuatro y media**
■ 5:35	**las cinco y treinta y cinco**
■ 11:45 A.M.	**las once y cuarenta y cinco**
	las doce menos cuarto A.M.
■ noon	**el mediodía**
■ midnight	**la medianoche**

When

■ today	**hoy**
■ morning	**la mañana**
■ afternoon/evening	**la tarde**
■ night	**la noche**
■ tonight	**esta noche**
■ there is/are	**hay**
■ ago	**hace**
■ an hour ago	**hace una hora**
■ a long time ago	**hace mucho tiempo**
■ not so long ago	**no hace mucho tiempo**
■ next month	**el próximo mes**
■ next summer	**el próximo verano**
■ next year	**el próximo año**
■ this weekend	**este fin de semana**
■ soon	**pronto**
■ yesterday	**ayer**
■ the day before	**anteayer**
■ that day	**ese día**
■ at that moment	**en ese momento**
■ tomorrow	**mañana**
■ the day after	**pasado mañana**

Weather/Climate

NOTES
Weather = **El Tiempo**
Climate = **El Clima**

Examples:
- "How is the weather?"
  "¿Qué tiempo hace?"

- "What is the temperature?"
  "¿Cuál es la temperatura?"

- "It's 20 degrees this morning."
  "Hace veinte grados esta mañana."

■ We're having bad weather	**hace mal tiempo**
■ it's beautiful/nice	**hace buen tiempo**
■ beauty	**la belleza**
■ it's cloudy	**está nublado**
■ cloud	**la nube**
■ it's cold	**hace frío**
■ cold	**frío**
■ it's cool	**hace fresco**
■ coolness	**la frescura**
■ inside	**adentro**
■ it's 15 degrees	**hace quince grados**

■ it's freezing	**hiela**
■ frost	**la escarcha**
■ hail	**el granizo**
■ it's hot	**hace calor**
■ heat	**el calor**
■ it's humid	**está húmedo**
■ humidity	**la humedad**
■ ice	**el hielo**
■ it's lightning	**hay relámpagos**
■ lightning	**el relámpago**
■ it's a full moon	**es la luna llena**
■ moon	**la luna**
■ outside	**afuera**
■ it's overcast	**está nublado**
■ it's raining	**llueve**
■ rain	**la lluvia**
■ sky	**el cielo**
■ it's snowing	**nieva**
■ snow	**la nieve**
■ it's stormy	**hay tormenta**
■ storm	**tormenta**
■ it's sunny	**hace sol**
■ sun	**el sol**
■ it's thundering	**está tronando**
■ thunder	**el trueno**
■ it's windy	**está ventoso**
■ wind	**el viento**

Habitat

Examples:
- "Where do you live?"
  "¿Dónde vive usted?"

For plurals, add "**s**" unless the word ends in a consonant, in which case add "**es**."

■ agency	**la agencia**
■ alarm clock	**el despertador**
■ apartment	**el apartamento**
■ artist studio	**el taller**
■ balcony	**el balcón**
■ bathroom	**el cuarto de baño**
■ bathroom sink	**el lavamanos**
■ bathtub	**la bañera**
■ bed	**la cama**
■ bedroom	**la habitación**
■ bedsheet	**la sábana**
■ bedside table	**la mesa de noche**
■ blanket	**la manta**

■ building	**el edificio**
■ calculator	**la calculadora**
■ chair	**la silla**
■ city	**la ciudad**
■ closet	**el armario**
■ compact disk	**el disco compacto**
■ computer	**el ordenador**
■ courtyard	**el patio**
■ cupboard	**el armario**
■ curtain	**la cortina**
■ desk	**el escritorio**
■ dining room	**el comedor**
■ door	**la puerta**
■ downtown	**el centro de la ciudad**
■ drinkable water	**el agua potable**
■ electricity	**la electricidad**
■ elevator	**el ascensor**
■ entrance	**la entrada**
■ first floor	**la planta baja**
■ floor	**el piso**
■ furniture	**los muebles**
■ garage	**el garaje**
■ gas (cooking)	**el gas**
■ hallway	**el pasillo**
■ heating (central)	**la calefacción central**
■ hotel	**el hotel**
■ hot plate	**el calentador**
■ house	**la casa**
■ kitchen	**la cocina**
■ lamp	**la lámpara**
■ landlord/landlady	**el propietario/a**
■ living room	**la sala de estar**
■ mattress	**el colchón**

■ mirror	**el espejo**
■ neighborhood	**la vecindad**
■ photograph	**la fotografía**
■ pillow	**el almohadón**
■ plant	**la planta**
■ poster	**el cartel**
■ radiator	**el radiador**
■ real estate	**el inmobiliario**
■ real estate agency	**la agencia inmobliaria**
■ recycling	**el reciclaje**
■ refrigerator	**la nevera**
■ -to rent	**alquilar**
■ rent	**el alquiler**
■ room	**el cuarto**
■ rug	**la alfombra**
■ shower	**la ducha**
■ smoke	**el humo**
■ sofa	**el sofá**
■ staircase	**la escalera**
■ stereo system	**el estéreo**
■ street	**la calle**
■ studio apartment	**el estudio**
■ suburb	**el suburbio**
■ telephone	**el teléfono**
■ television	**la televisión**
■ terrace	**la terraza**
■ toilet	**el inodoro**
■ towel	**la toalla**
■ wall	**la pared**
■ waste basket	**el cesto para papeles**

The Family

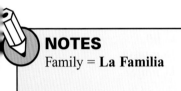

NOTES
Family = **La Familia**

For plurals, add "**s**" unless the word ends in a consonant, in which case add "**es**."

■ aunt	**la tía**
■ best friend	**el/la mejor amigo/a**
■ brother	**el hermano**
■ child	**el/la niño/a**
■ cousin	**el/la primo/a**
■ daughter	**la hija**
■ father	**el padre**
■ father-in-law	**el suegro**
■ friend	**el/la amigo/a**
■ grandchild/grandson	**el nieto**
■ granddaughter	**la nieta**
■ grandfather	**el abuelo**
■ grandmother	**la abuela**
■ grandparents	**los abuelos**
■ husband	**el marido**
■ mother	**la madre**
■ mother-in-law	**la suegra**
■ nephew	**el sobrino**

■ niece	**la sobrina**
■ parents	**los padres**
■ relatives	**los parientes**
■ sister	**la hermana**
■ stepfather	**el padrastro**
■ stepmother	**la madrastra**
■ son	**el hijo**
■ twin	**el/la gemelo/a**
■ uncle	**el tío**
■ wife	**la esposa**
■ woman	**la mujer**

31 People/ The Person

NOTES
People = **La Gente**
Person = **La Persona**

Examples:
- "What is your name?"
  "¿Cómo se llama?"

- Mrs.   **señora**
- Ms./Miss   **señorita**
- Mr.   **señor**
- -to like   **gustar**
- -to love   **querer**
- -to be in love   **estar enamorado/a**
- -to fall in love   **enamorarse**
- honeymoon   **la luna de miel**

The Body

32

NOTES

The Body = **El Cuerpo**

Examples:
- "I feel great."
  "Me siento muy bien."
- "I feel sick."
  "Me siento enfermo/a."
- "It burns!"
  "¡Me quema!"
- "Rest!"
  "¡Descanse!"
- "Where does it hurt?"
  "¿Dónde duele?"
- "You look sick."
  "Parece que usted está enfermo/a."

■ -to be cold	**tener frío**
■ -to have a headache	**tener dolor de cabeza**
■ -to be hot	**tener calor**
■ -to be hungry	**tener hambre**
■ -to hurt	**doler**
■ -to be sleepy	**estar soñoliento/a**
■ -to sprain	**torcerse**

113

■ -to have a stomachache	**tener dolor de estómago**
■ -to get a sunburn	**tener una quemadura de sol**
■ -to be thirsty	**tener sed**
■ -to have a toothache	**tener dolor de muelas**
■ -to be 20-years-old	**tener veinte años**
■ ankle	**el tobillo**
■ arm	**el brazo**
■ back	**la espalda**
■ belly	**el vientre**
■ ear	**la oreja**
■ eye	**el ojo**
■ eyebrow	**la ceja**
■ finger	**el dedo**
■ foot	**el pie**
■ hand	**la mano**
■ hair	**el cabello**
■ heart	**el corazón**
■ knee	**la rodilla**
■ leg	**la pierna**
■ lip	**el labio**
■ liver	**el hígado**
■ lung	**el pulmón**
■ mouth	**la boca**
■ neck	**el cuello**
■ nose	**la nariz**
■ shoulder	**el hombro**
■ stomach	**el estómago**
■ throat	**la garganta**
■ toe	**el dedo del pie**
■ tooth	**el diente**
■ wrist	**la muñeca**

NOTES
Health = **La Salud**

■ antibiotic	**el antibiótico**
■ antiseptic	**el antiséptico**
■ aspirin	**la aspirina**
■ blood	**la sangre**
■ bronchitis	**la bronquitis**
■ burn	**la quemadura**
■ cast	**el yeso**
■ cold	**el resfriado**
■ cough	**la tos**
■ cough syrup	**el jarabe para la tos**
■ death	**la muerte**
■ diagnostic	**el diagnóstico**
■ diet	**la dieta**
■ doctor	**el doctor**
■ drop	**la gota**
■ fever	**la fiebre**
■ flu	**la gripe**
■ herbal tea	**el té de hierbas**
■ illness	**la enfermedad**
■ indigestion	**la indigestión**
■ infection	**la infección**

■ injection	**la inyección**
■ medicine (drug)	**el medicamento**
■ nausea	**la náusea**
■ ointment	**el ungüento**
■ pain	**el dolor**
■ patient	**el paciente**
■ penicillin	**la penicilina**
■ pharmacy	**la farmacia**
■ prescription	**la receta**
■ remedy	**el remedio**
■ shot	**la inyección**
■ sickness	**la enfermedad**
■ sore throat	**el dolor de garganta**
■ sunburn	**la quemadura de sol**
■ swollen	**hinchado/a**
■ syrup	**el jarabe**
■ thermometer	**el termómetro**
■ temperature	**la temperatura**
■ toothache	**el dolor de muelas**
■ tonsillitis	**la amigdalitis**

34 Studies & the Workplace

Examples:
- "Study!"
  "¡Estudie usted!"
- "Work!"
  "¡Trabaje usted!"
- to complete a degree in French
  obtener un título en francés
- to earn money
  ganar dinero
- to study
  estudiar
- to take a course
  tomar un curso

For the plural form, add an **"s"** at the end, unless the word ends in a consonant, in which case add **"es."**

■ accountant	**el contador**
■ actor/actress	**el actor/la actriz**
■ accounting	**la contabilidad**
■ advertising	**la publicidad**

■ anthropology	**la antropología**
■ architect	**el arquitecto**
■ arts	**las artes**
■ astronomy	**la astronomía**
■ atlas	**el atlas**
■ B.A/B.S degree	**el título de bachiller**
	en artes/ciencias
■ biography	**la biografía**
■ biology	**la biología**
■ book	**el libro**
■ bookstore	**la librería**
■ botany	**la botánica**
■ business studies	**los estudios de negocio**
■ campus	**el campo**
■ career	**la carrera**
■ chemistry	**la química**
■ colleague	**el colega**
■ college	**la universidad**
■ computer	**el ordenador**
■ computer lab	**el laboratorio de informática**
■ computer science	**la informática**
■ course	**el curso**
■ degree	**el título**
■ dentist	**el dentista**
■ dictionary	**el diccionario**
■ dining hall	**el comedor**
■ doctor	**el doctor**
■ drawing	**el dibujo**
■ economics	**la economía**
■ education	**la educación**
■ encyclopedia	**la enciclopedia**
■ engineer	**el ingeniero**
■ enrollment	**la inscripción**

■ exam	**el exámen**
■ factory	**la fábrica**
■ fine arts	**las bellas artes**
■ foreign languages	**los idiomas extranjeros**
■ full-time	**el período completo**
■ geography	**la geografía**
■ geology	**la geología**
■ grade	**la calificación**
■ gymnasium	**el gimnasio**
■ health clinic	**la enfermería**
■ history	**la historia**
■ hospital	**el hospital**
■ humanities	**las humanidades**
■ job	**el trabajo**
■ journalism	**el periodismo**
■ journalist	**el periodista**
■ laboratory	**el laboratorio**
■ language lab	**el laboratorio de idiomas**
■ law	**el derecho**
■ law school	**la escuela de derecho**
■ lawyer	**el abogado**
■ lecture hall	**el salónde conferencias**
■ liberal arts	**las artes liberales**
■ library	**la biblioteca**
■ linguistics	**la lingüística**
■ literature	**la literatura**
■ major	**la especialización**
■ mathematics	**las matemáticas**
■ mechanic	**el mecánico**
■ medicine	**la medicina**
■ money	**el dinero**
■ music	**la música**
■ musician	**el músico**

■ natural sciences	**las ciencias naturales**
■ nurse	**la/el enfermera/o**
■ office	**la oficina**
■ painter	**el pintor**
■ painting	**la pintura**
■ part-time	**tiempo parcial**
■ pharmacist	**el farmacéutico/a**
■ philosophy	**la filosofía**
■ physics	**la física**
■ poetry	**la poesía**
■ political sciences	**las ciencias politicas**
■ police officer	**el oficial de policía**
■ professor	**el/la profesor(a)**
■ psychology	**la psicología**
■ report	**la información de noticias**
■ schedule	**el horario**
■ school	**la escuela**
■ secretary	**la secretaria**
■ semester	**el semestre**
■ sociology	**la sociología**
■ social worker	**el asistente social**
■ stadium	**el estadio**
■ studies	**los estudios**
■ teacher (elementary)	**el/la maestro/a**
■ technician	**el técnico**
■ theater	**el teatro**
■ trimester	**el trimestre**
■ waiter/waitress	**el camarero/a**
■ work	**el trabajo**
■ writer	**el escritor**
■ work (full-time)	**trabajo a tiempo completo**
■ work (part-time)	**trabajo a tiempo parcial**
■ zoology	**la zoología**

35 Computer

NOTES
Computer = **El Ordenador** *or* **la Computadora**

■ CD-ROM drive	**el mando CD-ROM**
■ computer file	**el fichero**
■ database	**la base de datos**
■ electronic mail	**el correo electrónico**
■ floppy disk	**el disco flexible**
■ hard drive	**el disco duro**
■ keyboard	**el teclado**
■ monitor	**el monitor**
■ mouse	**el ratón**
■ network	**la red**
■ portable computer	**el ordenador portátil**
■ printer	**la impresora**
■ program	**el programa**
■ -to save	**salvar, guardar**
■ screen	**la pantalla**
■ technology	**la tecnología**
■ word processing	**el tratamiento de texto**

121

Sports & Entertainment

Examples:
- "I am having fun!"
  "¡Me estoy divirtiendo!"

- "I love vacations!"
  "¡Me encantan las vacaciones!"

- ■-to play the accordion **tocar el acordeón**
- ■-to go to the beach **ir a la playa**
- ■-to ride a bike **montar en bicicleta**
- ■-to go camping **ir a acampar**
- ■-to go to a concert **ir a un concierto**
- ■-to play dominos **jugar al dominó**
- ■-to spend a quiet evening **pasar una tarde tranquila**
- ■-to do exercises **hacer ejercicios**
- ■-to see an exhibition **ir a ver una exposición**
- ■-to go fishing **ir de pesca**
- ■-to take a hike **hacer una caminata**
- ■-to go horseback riding **montar a caballo**

■ -to go jogging	**trotar**
■ -to go motorcycle riding	**montar en motocicleta**
■ -to go mountain climbing	**hacer el alpinismo**
■ -to perform in a play	**actuar en una obra de teatro**
■ -to play rugby	**jugar al rugby**
■ -to run	**correr**
■ -to go sailing	**pasear en barco de vela**
■ -to (ice) skate	**patinar**
■ -to ski	**esquiar**
■ -to swim	**nadar**
■ -to go on vacation	**ir de vacaciones**
■ -to walk	**caminar**
■ -to take a walk	**pasear**
■ -to waterski	**hacer el esquí acuático**
■ -to windsurf	**hacer surf a vela**

For the plural form, add an "**s**" at the end, unless the word ends in a consonant, in which case, add "**es**."

■ basketball	**baloncesto**
■ broadcast (a program)	**difundir**
■ camping	**el camping**
■ cards	**los naipes**
■ cartoon	**los dibujos animados**
■ cassette player	**el grabador de casete**
■ checkers	**el juego de damas**
■ chess	**el ajedrez**
■ comedy	**la comedia**
■ concert	**el concierto**
■ documentary	**el documental**

■ game	**el juego**
■ golf	**el golf**
■ guitar	**la guitarra**
■ jazz	**el jazz**
■ mountain bike	**la bicicleta de montaña**
■ mountain climbing	**el alpinismo**
■ movie	**la película**
■ movie star	**la estrella de cine**
■ movie theater	**el cine**
■ museum	**el museo**
■ music	**la música**
■ news	**el noticiero**
■ opera	**la ópera**
■ party	**la fiesta**
■ piano	**el piano**
■ place	**el lugar**
■ play	**la representación**
■ race	**la carrera**
■ radio	**la radio**
■ remote control	**el control remoto**
■ rest	**el descanso**
■ rock	**el rock**
■ rugby	**el rugby**
■ seat	**el asiento**
■ screen	**la pantalla**
■ soap opera	**la novela**
■ sport	**el deporte**
■ soccer	**el fútbol**
■ tape recorder	**la grabadora de cintas**
■ television	**la televisión**
■ tennis	**el tenis**
■ theater	**el teatro**
■ ticket	**el billete**

■ TV station — **la estación de televisión**
■ swimming pool — **la piscina**
■ vacation — **las vacaciones**
■ videocassette — **el videocasete**
■ video player — **el lector de video**

37 Food & Restaurant

NOTES
Food = **La Comida**
Restaurant = **El Restaurante**

Examples:
- "I would like..."
  "Me gustaría..."

- "I would like to order, please."
  "Me gustaría pedir, por favor."

- "The check please!"
  "¡La cuenta, por favor!"

- "Is the service included?"
  "¿Está el servicio incluido?"

For the plural form, add an "**s**" at the end, unless the word ends in a consonant, in which case, add "**es**."

- ◼ appetizer   **el aperitivo**
- ◼ bread   **el pan**
- ◼ breakfast   **el desayuno**
- ◼ butter   **la mantequilla**
- ◼ cake   **el pastel**
- ◼ candy   **el caramelo**

■ cheese	**el queso**
■ chocolate	**el chocolate**
■ cup	**la taza**
■ egg	**el huevo**
■ fork	**el tenedor**
■ french fries	**las papas fritas**
■ glass	**el vaso**
■ hamburger	**la hamburguesa**
■ knife	**el cuchillo**
■ lunch	**el almuerzo**
■ meal	**la comida**
■ mustard	**la mostaza**
■ napkin	**la servilleta**
■ oil	**el aceite**
■ pasta	**las pastas**
■ pepper	**la pimienta**
■ pizza	**la pizza**
■ rice	**el arroz**
■ salt	**la sal**
■ sandwich	**el sándwich**
■ snack	**el refrigerio**
■ spices	**las especias**
■ tip	**la propina**
■ vinegar	**el vinagre**

Desserts

■ cake	**el pastel**
■ chocolate	**el chocolate**
■ cookie	**la galleta**
■ cream	**la crema**
■ doughnut	**el buñuelo**
■ ice cream	**el helado**
■ tart	**la tarta**

Drinks

■ beer	**la cerveza**
■ bottle	**la botella**
■ dark beer	**la cerveza negra**
■ light beer	**la cerveza ligera**
■ coffee	**el café**
■ hot chocolate	**el chocolate caliente**
■ ice	**el hielo**
■ lemonade	**la limonada**
■ milk	**la leche**
■ orange juice	**el jugo de naranja**
■ soda	**el refresco**
■ diet soda	**el refresco de dieta**
■ tea	**el té**
■ water(iced)	**el agua helada**
■ wine	**el vino**
■ red wine	**el vino tinto**
■ rose wine	**el vino rosado**
■ white wine	**el vino blanco**

Fish

■ lobster	**la langosta**
■ shrimp	**el camarón**
■ tuna	**el atún**
■ salmon	**el salmón**
■ sole	**el lenguado**
■ trout	**la trucha**

Fruits

■ apple	**la manzana**
■ apricot	**el albaricoque**
■ avocado	**el aguacate**

- banana   **la banana**
- cherry   **la cereza**
- grapefruit   **la toronja**
- grapes   **las uvas**
- lemon   **el limón**
- mango   **el mango**
- olive   **la aceituna**
- orange   **la naranja**
- pear   **la pera**
- raspberry   **la frambuesa**
- strawberry   **la fresa**

Meat
- beef   **la carne de vaca**
- chicken   **el pollo**
- chop   **la chuleta**
- gravy   **la salsa**
- ham   **el jamón**
- turkey   **el pavo**
- veal   **la carne de ternera**

Vegetables
- beans   **los frijoles**
- beet   **la remolacha**
- broccoli   **el brócoli**
- cabbage   **la col**
- carrot   **la zanahoria**
- celery   **el apio**
- corn   **el maíz**
- cucumber   **el pepino**
- eggplant   **la berenjena**
- endive   **la endivia**
- green beans   **las judías**

■ lettuce	**la lechuga**
■ mushroom	**el hongo**
■ onion	**la cebolla**
■ peas	**las arvejas**
■ potato	**la papa**
■ pumpkin	**la calabaza**
■ spinach	**la espinaca**
■ zucchini	**el calabacín**

NOTES

Desserts = **Los Postres**

Drinks = **Las Bebidas**

Fish = **El Pescado**

Fruits = **Las Frutas**

Meat = **La Carne**

Vegetables = **Las Legumbres**

Questions & Negatives

NOTES
Questions = **Las Preguntas**
Negatives = **Los Negativos**

Questions

■ Is it...?	**¿Es eso?**
■ How?	**¿Cómo?**
■ How many/much?	**¿Cuánto?**
■ What?	**¿Qué?**
■ When?	**¿Cuándo?**
■ Where?	**¿Dónde?**
■ Which?	**¿Cuál(es)?**
■ Which one?	**¿Cuál?**
■ Which ones?	**¿Cuáles?**
■ Who?	**¿Quién?**
■ Why?	**¿Por qué?**

Negatives

■ not	**no**
■ never	**jamás**
■ no more	**no más**
■ nothing	**nada**
■ no one	**nadie**
■ not at all	**de ningún modo**

- not too much   **no demasiado**
- not much   **no mucho**
- not enough   **no bastante**
- not often   **no a menudo**
- not yet   **no aún**